D0500899

Mar 19

SHAPE YOUR OPINION

Should Kids Wear School Uniforms?

by Janie Havemeyer

NORWOODHOUSE PRESS

Norwood House Press
P.O. Box 316598
Chicago, Illinois 60631

For information regarding Norwood House Press, please visit our website at:
www.norwoodhousepress.com or call 866-565-2900.

PHOTO CREDITS: Cover Photo: © Monkey Business Images/Shutterstock Images; © aleksokolov/
iStockphoto, 21; © davidf/iStockphoto, 17, 18, 27; © Highwaystarz-Photography/iStockphoto,
34, 39; © Karpova/Shutterstock Images, 14; © michaeljung/iStockphoto, 12; © Monkey Business
Images/Shutterstock Images, 37; © SolStock/iStockphoto, 4, 32; © SpeedKingz/Shutterstock
Images, 24; © Steve Debenport/iStockphoto, 7; © wavebreakmedia/Shutterstock Images, 10

Hardcover ISBN: 978-1-59953-929-4
Paperback ISBN: 978-1-68404-201-2

© 2019 by Norwood House Press.

Library of Congress Cataloging-in-Publication Data

Names: Havemeyer, Janie, author.
Title: Should kids wear school uniforms? / by Janie Havemeyer.
Description: Chicago, Illinois : Norwood House Press, [2018] | Series: Shape your opinion |
    Includes bibliographical references and index.
Identifiers: LCCN 2018006096 (print) | LCCN 2018003234 (ebook) | ISBN 9781684042081 (ebook)
    | ISBN 9781599539294 (hardcover : alk. paper) | ISBN 9781684042012 (pbk. : alk. paper)
Subjects: LCSH: Students--United States--Uniforms. | Dress codes--United States.
Classification: LCC LB3024 (print) | LCC LB3024 .H38 2018 (ebook) | DDC 371.5/1--dc23
LC record available at https://lccn.loc.gov/2018006096

312N—072018
Manufactured in the United States of America in North Mankato, Minnesota.

Table of Contents

Students in some schools are required to wear uniforms.

1

What's the Issue with School Uniforms?

A school uniform is a special outfit students are required to wear at some schools. Students can sometimes choose from a few options. They might choose a light blue or white shirt. They might choose blue or black pants. Boys and girls may have different uniforms.

For many years, most **public schools** did not have uniforms. Uniforms were more common in **private schools**. A change happened in 1994. One California public **school district** took a bold step. It required all students to wear uniforms.

It was the first time an entire school district did this. The community reacted strongly. Some people liked the idea. Others were not happy.

The Rule Is Backed by Law

The school district was in Long Beach, California. The rule was for all students from kindergarten through eighth grade. Some families did not like uniforms. They said public schools should not decide what children could wear. They fought the rule. Some families decided to **sue** the school district. But California created a new law. The law said public schools could require uniforms. Students had no choice.

Supporters of school uniforms believe they improve learning and behavior.

The President Weighs In

In 1996, President Bill Clinton spoke up. He was in favor of school uniforms. He visited Long Beach to hear from students and principals. After his visit, he said uniforms were a good idea.

People said they improved student behavior. Clinton felt schools should be able to require uniforms. He said students should "**evaluate** themselves by what they are on the inside instead of what they're wearing on the outside."[1]

Soon, even more public schools added uniforms. In 1997, clothing company Lands' End took notice. It started selling uniforms. Other companies followed. By 2013, one in five public schools required uniforms.

Why All the Fuss?

The school uniform debate stirs up strong feelings. Some people are strongly in favor of uniforms. Others are strongly against them. Fashion designer Joanne Arbuckle wore a uniform in school. She said uniforms made students feel as if they were prisoners. Still, schools may feel that uniforms are good for their students.

In Favor of Uniforms

People who like school uniforms think good things happen when students wear them. They say students show more school pride. Uniforms help students feel better about themselves. It is harder for students to label one

Some students don't like wearing a school uniform. They would rather choose their own clothes.

another based on clothing. Students focus on their work and not their clothes when everyone dresses alike. They behave better. Schools are safer.

Against Uniforms

People who don't like uniforms think differently. They say parents and students should decide about clothes. There should not be a required outfit. Students should be able to dress the way they want. They should be allowed to express themselves. Others say buying a school uniform is a waste of money. It is an outfit that can be worn only in school.

EXPLORE THIS BOOK

In this book, three questions about school uniforms will be examined. *Do school uniforms improve students' self-image? Do school uniforms help students learn? Do school uniforms improve school spirit?* Each chapter ends with a section called **Let's Look at the Opinions**. This section focuses on points to remember when forming an opinion. At the end of the book, students can test their skills at writing their own opinion essays.

Many students feel confident when wearing their school uniforms.

2

Do School Uniforms Improve Self-Image?

YES: Wearing a Uniform Improves Students' Self-Image

Students feel proud when they wear school uniforms. They feel they belong to something important. They are part of a group. Uniforms can cut down on teasing. No one is bullied because of his or her clothes. This leads to happier students. When students wear uniforms, they feel more confident about their appearance. They are also less distracted by the clothing of others.

Students want to feel good about the clothes they wear.

Clothes Send a Message

Even kids as young as six care about how they look. Ohio principal Joseph Copeland says uniforms help kids feel more equal. They also help students feel better about themselves. Clothes send out clues about who you are. Many kids know about popular clothing brands. They may want to wear these clothes. One student might wear clothes that cost a lot.

Another student might be embarrassed if her clothes are out of style. With uniforms, these differences go away. It is harder to see who can't afford popular clothes. There is no **peer pressure** to dress a certain way.

What Does a Uniform Say about You?

Dorothy Behling is an expert on how people think and act. She studied what students and teachers think when they see a person in a school uniform. Behling talked to people at two schools. She found that a uniform sends a message. People think a student wearing a uniform will do better in school. Schools sometimes say that students should "dress for success."

School uniforms help some students believe they can succeed.

When teachers believe students will do well, students believe it too. This gives students confidence. Students are dressing for success when they wear a uniform.

NO: Wearing a Uniform Does Not Improve Students' Self-Image

Uniforms do not fit all students the same way. People have different body types. A uniform may not come in the right size. It might be too short or too tight. Students may not like wearing a uniform that does not fit well.

Wearing a uniform can make it harder to do things like play sports.

A uniform that fits poorly can also affect how students move. One student said, "Uniforms are uncomfortable. They make you feel stiff like robots."[2] Not being able to move freely can make students feel awkward. It can harm their self-image.

Expressing Yourself

Choosing your clothing is a way to show who you are. A uniform might not match how a student feels inside. Wendy likes to wear T-shirts. But her school's uniform requires a blouse. Jerome likes to wear shorts. But he must wear long pants. These students may not like the way they look at school. If you don't like the way you look, you may not feel good about yourself.

Some kids may not like how they look or feel in their school uniforms.

Summing It Up!

People have strong feelings about the issue of school uniforms. Many principals think school uniforms help students feel better about themselves. This is a common reason for requiring uniforms. But not everyone agrees. Students may not like the way a uniform looks or feels. It may be uncomfortable. It may not match their style. If that happens, the student may not feel good.

Let's Look at the Opinions
ASKING PEOPLE'S OPINION

One way to support your opinion is to ask other people about their opinions. Experts sometimes give surveys. They ask a large group of people a question. Then they figure out what answers were most popular.

One argument mentioned an expert named Dorothy Behling. She found out what students and teachers think when they see a person wearing a school uniform. The people she asked went to two schools in Ohio. People in other states might have different thoughts.

Studies such as this one ask people's opinion. An opinion is one person's belief. When you read about a study, keep a few things in mind. Who was asked to share their opinion? Would other people, such as parents, think differently? What if the people came from a different state? Then decide if this study is the best one to support your opinion.

Some teachers think school uniforms have a positive effect on learning.

3

Do School Uniforms Help Students Learn?

YES: Wearing a Uniform Helps Students Learn

Some people say uniforms help students. Students are less distracted. Teachers can focus on teaching if students are focused on learning. Teachers don't waste time dealing with students with distracting clothing.

Getting to School

Uniforms make it easier to get ready for school. Students have fewer choices about what to wear.

That helps them get to school on time. They can focus on getting ready to learn instead of thinking about what to wear. A student in Massachusetts agrees. He believes it would take him less time to get ready for school if he had a uniform.

Some people believe uniforms make students more willing to go to school. Uniforms made a big difference at one school in California. Attendance reached a new record. The assistant principal thought kids were less afraid to come to school. They didn't have to worry about being teased about their clothes. If kids are worried about getting teased, they cannot learn well. Uniforms help them focus on school.

Some people think uniforms help students feel better about going to school.

NO: Wearing a Uniform Does Not Help Students Learn

Some people don't think uniforms help students learn. They don't think having everyone dress the same way makes a difference. Uniforms alone don't make students pay attention. Other people say uniforms get in the way of other school goals. Students are expected to share their opinions. Different opinions are valued. But when students dress alike, they may feel they should think alike, too. They might feel they should be like everyone else. A student wrote about this. She wondered how students could be themselves if the school tells them how to dress and act.

Where's the Proof?

Some people want proof that uniforms help students. Researchers have looked for evidence in students' test scores. They want to see if scores rise after a school requires uniforms. Another thing they look at is attendance. Do more students come to school after uniforms are introduced? Results have been mixed. They do not point to a clear answer.

David Brunsma has studied this issue. He works at a college and wrote a book about

Use of School Uniforms

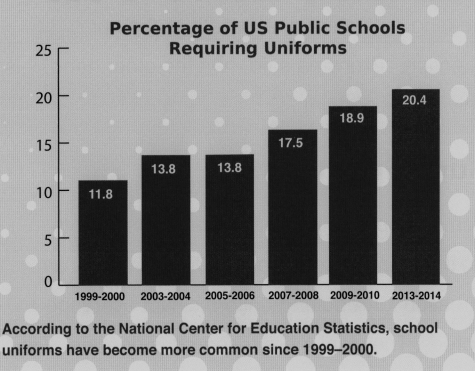

Percentage of US Public Schools Requiring Uniforms

Year	Percentage
1999-2000	11.8
2003-2004	13.8
2005-2006	13.8
2007-2008	17.5
2009-2010	18.9
2013-2014	20.4

According to the National Center for Education Statistics, school uniforms have become more common since 1999–2000.

school uniforms. He hasn't found evidence that uniforms help students. He thinks wearing a uniform is like putting a fresh coat of paint on an old house. The house might look better. But it might still have creaky floors and a broken window. A uniform might look good, too. But it doesn't change anything about the student wearing it. "On the one hand it grabs our attention," Brunsma said. "On the other hand, it is only a coat of paint."[3]

Summing It Up!

Some people believe uniforms help students do better in school. These people give this as a reason for requiring uniforms. Not everyone agrees. They feel more research is needed. It is not clear whether uniforms really help.

THE POWER OF A QUOTE

In this chapter, the author shares the opinion of David Brunsma. Brunsma works at a college. He says uniforms do not change anything about the students wearing them. His words are recorded in the form of a quote.

A quote is an exact version of what someone said. A writer may use one or more quotes to support an opinion. A good quote comes from a person who knows a lot about the subject. When considering whether to quote someone, make sure to ask questions. Why is this person speaking up? Is he or she an expert? Does he or she have something to gain? Keep these things in mind as you weigh his or her opinion. Does the person give facts to back up his or her opinion? Facts make opinions stronger. Asking these questions will help you pick the best quotes.

Supporters of school uniforms say school spirit improves when students dress alike.

4

Do School Uniforms Improve School Spirit?

YES: Wearing a Uniform Improves School Spirit

People who like uniforms compare a school to a team. School uniforms make students feel as if they are part of a team. A school uniform often has the school's colors on it. It may have school symbols sewn on. Students wearing school colors feel connected with their school. They feel connected with their fellow students. This may give students a stronger sense of belonging. Uniforms may give them more school spirit.

DID YOU KNOW?

An education group discovered that most principals think uniforms help their schools. About 85 percent thought students were better behaved. About 79 percent thought students were safer. And about 64 percent thought students got better grades.

What Do Teachers Say?

A group of more than 500 principals at schools with uniforms answered questions. They explained how uniforms changed their schools. More than three quarters said school pride improved.

Teachers have also noticed changes. One teacher said uniforms led to more school spirit.

Not all students feel more school spirit by wearing a uniform.

"Kids are talking about the school colors and the uniforms," he said.[4] Another teacher said students looked proud when wearing uniforms. The students looked like a team when they went on school trips.

NO: Wearing a Uniform Does Not Improve School Spirit

Some people don't agree that uniforms improve school spirit. They say students should choose their own clothes. Every student should have the right to dress the way he or she wants. Choosing clothes is a way for students to express themselves. Students won't feel more school spirit just because they are dressed alike.

Many students like to choose what they wear as a way of showing who they are.

What Do Students Say?

A school district in Maryland asked parents and students about uniforms. Parents strongly supported uniforms. More than half of parents favored uniforms. However, the students had much different opinions. Only 12 percent supported uniforms. Students argued that uniforms blocked **freedom of expression**. They wanted to show their personalities. Choosing their own clothes could help. Students who are forced to wear uniforms might be uncomfortable. They would feel less school spirit, not more.

The **US Constitution** gives all citizens certain rights. One of these is freedom of expression. This is the freedom to share your opinions and ideas. It includes dressing the way you want. People say the government shouldn't tell students what to wear.

Some studies show that parents favor school uniforms more than students do.

Summing It Up!

Most school leaders believe uniforms have a positive effect. They feel that wearing uniforms gives students more school spirit. But some students and parents feel that uniforms stop students from expressing themselves. This can stop students from feeling school spirit.

USING COMPARISONS

Writers use different methods to explain their opinions. One is using comparisons. The author compares a school uniform to a sports uniform. Players wear uniforms to show which team they are on. By comparing the two, the author makes a point. School uniforms make students feel part of a team. In both cases, uniforms help to build pride and spirit.

The author also presents a teacher's opinion. The teacher talks about what she noticed when the school required uniforms. She felt the students looked as if they were part of a team. Using comparisons can help people understand the argument you are making. This may work to sway others to agree with your point of view.

Write What You Think!

The author shares different opinions in this book. Some opinions state why school uniforms are good for students. Other opinions argue that uniforms don't help. It's important to know many sides of an argument before you form your own opinion.

Opinion writing has a purpose. The writer tries to convince the reader to agree with his or her point of view through different writing methods. One method is to use polls or research results. Another method is to refer to the endorsement of an expert or a well-known person. Yet another method is to compare one thing to another. All these methods help make a stronger point.

In writing your own opinion piece, here are six steps to follow:

Step One: *Choose what to write about.*

Pick a subject that interests you. Now think of a question you have about that subject. Decide how you would answer the question. Which side are you on?

Step Two: *Find out more.*

Before you write, find out more about your subject. Read what other people have to say. You could take a poll. In this book, poll results were reported. Principals and students gave their opinions. Ask other people what they think, especially if they know a lot about a subject. Find out the facts. See if an expert has something to say on the subject.

Step Three: *State your opinion.*

The first few sentences should say what your paper is about. You may want to include a question. For example, you could start this way: "This essay is about school uniforms. It asks the question, Should school uniforms be required?"

Next, write down your opinion. You can use phrases such as *I think, I believe,* or *in my opinion.* Examples are:

- I think students should wear uniforms.
- I believe students should choose what clothes to wear to school.
- In my opinion, there are many benefits to students wearing school uniforms.

Step Four: *Give reasons.*

Opinions should be followed up with reasons for those opinions. Logical reasons can influence others to think like you. Come up with two or three reasons why you think the way you do about your subject. Write each reason in a sentence. Use linking words like *because, since,* and *therefore* to connect your opinion with the reasons why you came to a certain conclusion. For example, if you are writing a piece on whether students should wear school uniforms or choose their own school clothes, you might give these reasons:

- I think choosing your own clothes is important, *since* students should have the right to decide how to dress and think.
- I think students should wear school uniforms *because* then no one has to worry about what to wear to school.

Step Five: *Support your reasons.*

The opinion of a famous person or an authority is a good way to back up your reason. So are results from a survey or research study. Here is an example of how to do this:

First, give an opinion with a reason:

- I think choosing your own clothes is important, since students should have the right to decide how to dress and think.

Then, give a fact to back up the reason:

- Surveys show that most students agree.

Step Six: *Write the ending.*

Summarize your opinion in the last sentence or two. This makes it clear for the reader what side you are on and why you think the way you do. A good summary wraps up your argument and helps convince the reader to think as you do. You could begin the last sentence with any of these phrases, or you can think of your own:

- For all these reasons, . . .
- As the survey results indicate, . . .
- To sum up, . . .

GLOSSARY

evaluate (ih-VAL-yoo-ate): To judge the value of someone or something in a careful way.

freedom of expression (FREE-dum uv ik-SPRESH-un): The right of someone to freely present his or her ideas and opinions through speech, in writing, or in other ways.

peer pressure (PEER presh-er): A feeling that you must do the same things as other people your age.

private schools (PRY-vit skoolz): Schools that are not run by the government. They cost money to attend.

public schools (PUB-lick skoolz): Schools that are run by the government. They are free to attend.

school district (SKOOL dis-trikt): A group of schools in an area that are operated by one administration.

sue (SOO): To get a court to decide if you are being treated unfairly.

US Constitution (YOU-ess con-stuh-TOO-shun): A document that describes the government of the United States and lists some of the rights of its people.

BIBLIOGRAPHY

Books

Carole, Bonnie. *School Uniforms, Yes or No.* Vero Beach, FL: Rourke Educational Media, 2015.

Kawa, Katie. *Are School Uniforms Good for Students?* New York: KidHaven Publishing, 2018.

Websites

National Survey of School Leaders Reveals 2013 School Uniform Trends

naesp.org/sites/default/files/UniformsInforgraphic_compressed.pdf

Students Voice Opinions over Uniforms

wareham-ma.villagesoup.com/p/students-voice-opinions-over-uniforms/1113636

SOURCE NOTES

1. Alison Mitchell. "Clinton Will Advise Schools on Uniforms." *New York Times.* The New York Times Company, 25 Feb. 1996. Web. 4 Jan. 2018.

2. Debra Viadero. "Uniform Effects?" *Education Week.* Editorial Projects in Education, 12 Jan. 2005. Web. 25 Oct. 2017.

3. David L. Brunsma. *The School Uniform Movement and What It Tells Us about American Education.* Lanham, MD: Scarecrow Education, 2004. Print. 48.

4. John A. Huss. "The Role of School Uniforms in Creating an Academically Motivating Climate: Do Uniforms Influence Teacher's Expectations?" *Journal of Ethnographic & Qualitative Research.* Winter 2007, vol. 1. Web. 4 Jan. 2018.

Index

About the Author

Janie Havemeyer is an author of many books for children. Janie loves learning about issues and understanding different points of view. She is a graduate of Middlebury College and Bank Street Graduate School of Education. For many years, Janie taught in elementary schools and in art museums.